Where's
My Cheese

Where's My Cheese?

by Stan Mack!

Pantheon Books

for Jane

J

M

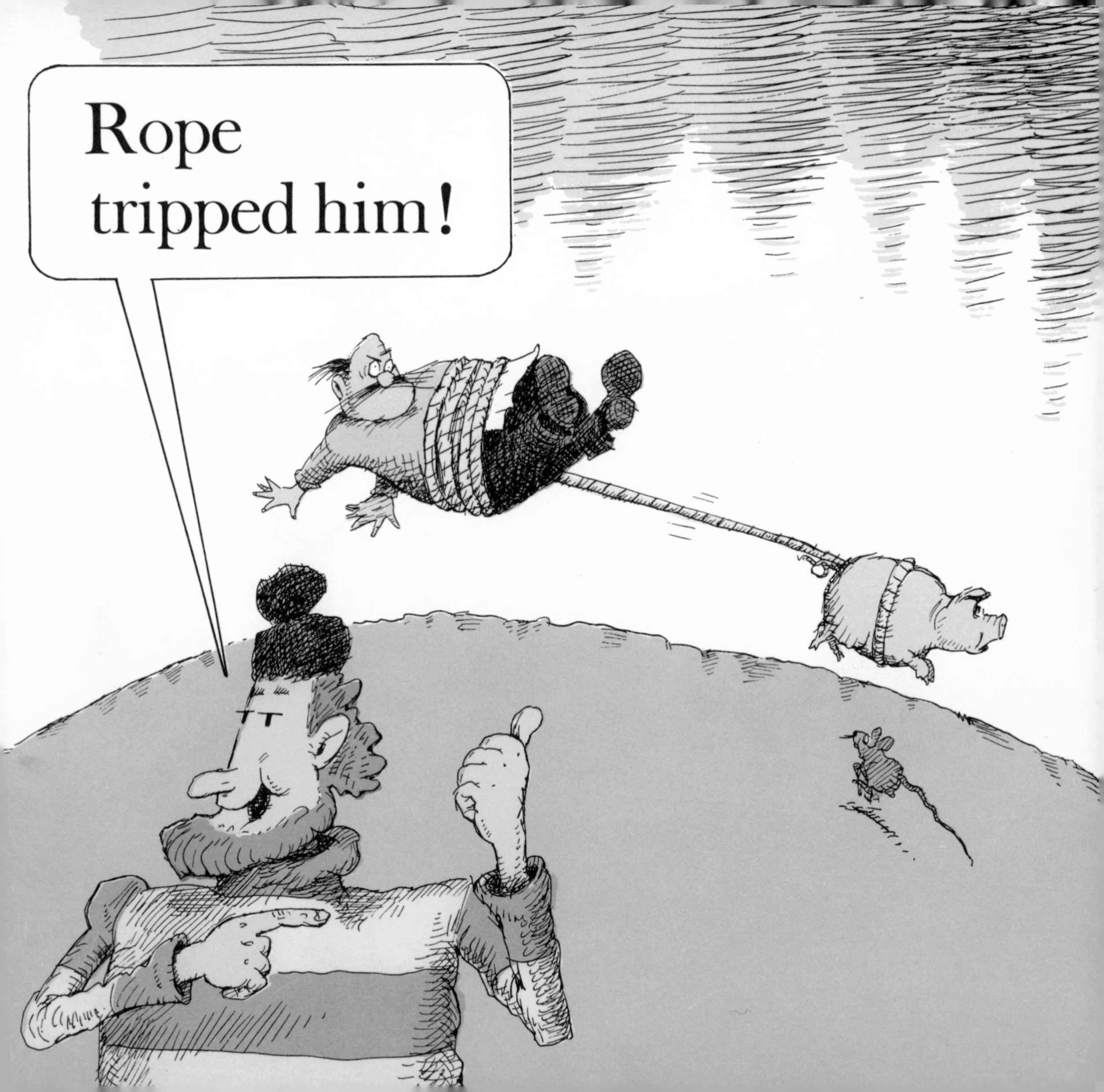
Rope tripped him!

From his pictures for *The Brownstone* ("Easy to look at, to listen to, to read, and to smile over." *Library Journal*), to those in *The King's Cat Is Coming*, Stan Mack's comical characters are growing increasingly popular with picture book audiences.

He has also created a prize-winning film for The Children's Television Workshop and wrote and illustrated *10 Bears in My Bed*, selected by *The New York Times* as among the best of 1974.

Based on an old choosing game, *Where's My Cheese?* is a 1977 Junior Literary Guild selection.